SNEAKY SHARKS

HERE'S HOW TO MAKE THE MOST OF YOUR
SUPER-COOL LEGO® BOOK . . .

1.
BUILD YOUR BRAND
NEW LEGO MINIFIGURE.
IT'S THE DAREDEVIL STUNTMAN
JETT POWERS, TO ADD TO
YOUR COLLECTION!

2.
READ THE STORY
OF HOW THE LEGO CITY
PEOPLE GET ONE OVER ON
A GANG OF THIEVES.

3.
SOLVE THE PUZZLES
AND HELP THE STUNTMEN
SAVE THE DAY!

SEARCH AND FIND

Get yourself an ice cream – you're at LEGO CITY Beach! Can you find all of the characters from our story in this busy seaside scene?

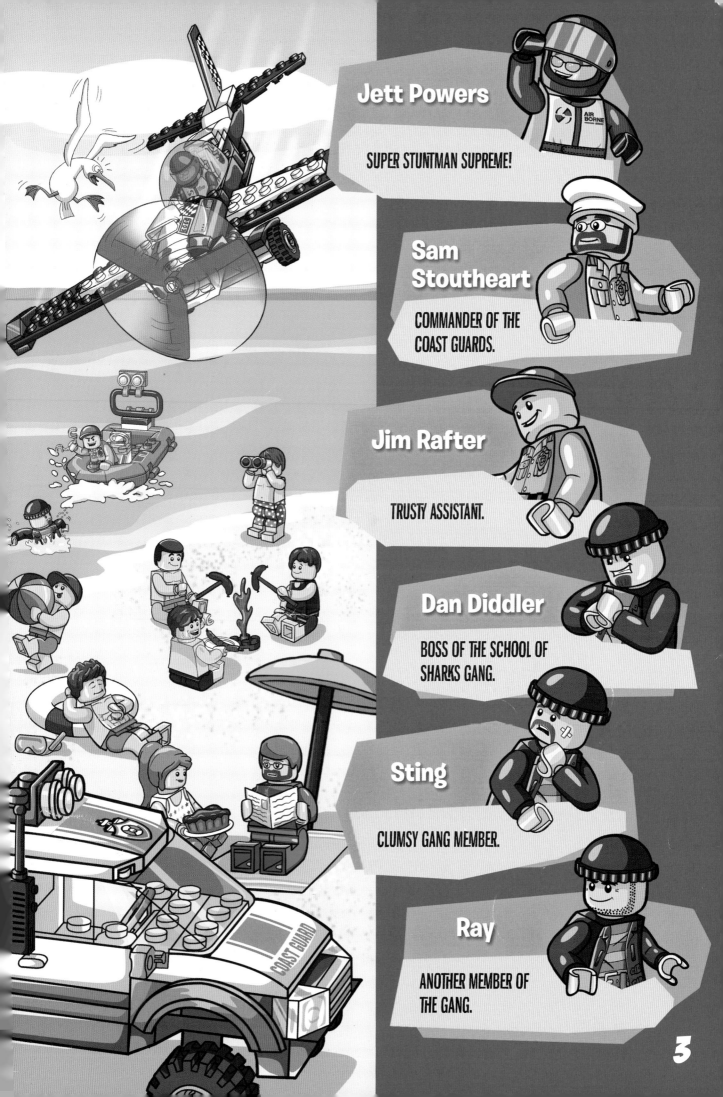

Jett Powers

SUPER STUNTMAN SUPREME!

Sam Stoutheart

COMMANDER OF THE COAST GUARDS.

Jim Rafter

TRUSTY ASSISTANT.

Dan Diddler

BOSS OF THE SCHOOL OF SHARKS GANG.

Sting

CLUMSY GANG MEMBER.

Ray

ANOTHER MEMBER OF THE GANG.

A FISHY TALE

LEGO CITY Beach was packed with people, all staring up at the sky. They were waiting for the daredevil Jett Powers to arrive in his Super Soarer stunt plane.

"Jett Powers is so lucky," sighed coast guard assistant Jim Rafter. "He works in the sky!"

"We work in the sea," replied the head coast guard, Sam Stoutheart. "That's pretty cool too. Now, keep your eyes off the skies. Remember, it's our job to watch the people and make sure they stay safe."

"Aye aye, Commander," said Jim.

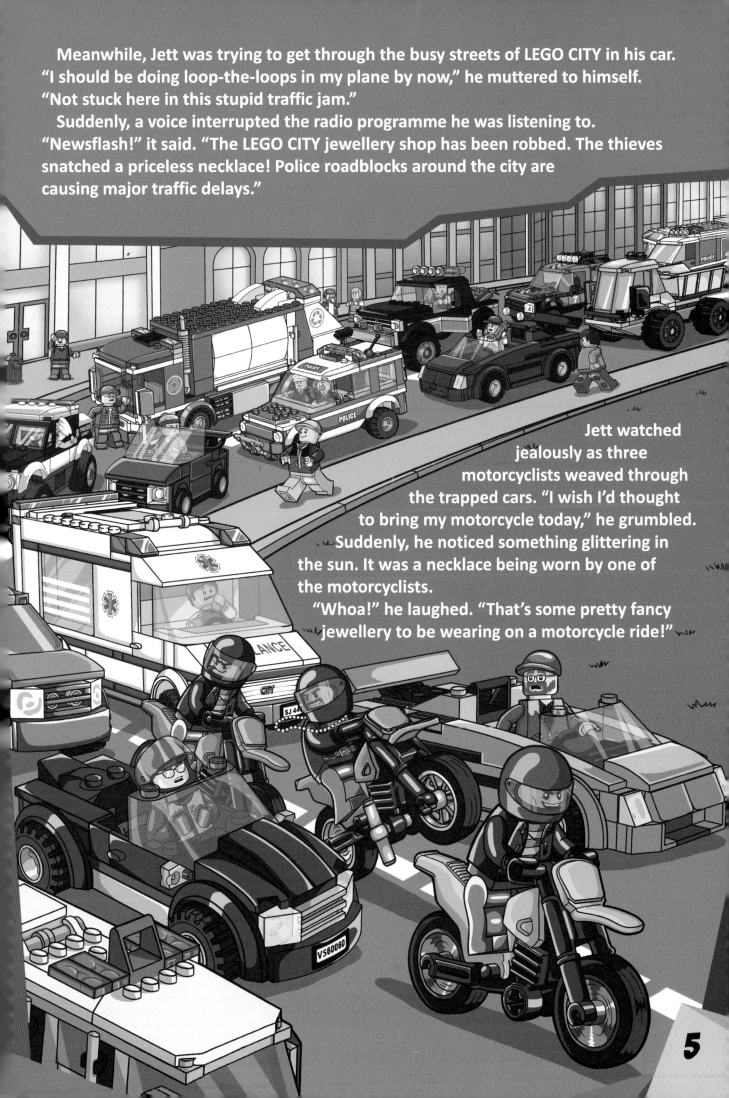

Meanwhile, Jett was trying to get through the busy streets of LEGO CITY in his car. "I should be doing loop-the-loops in my plane by now," he muttered to himself. "Not stuck here in this stupid traffic jam."

Suddenly, a voice interrupted the radio programme he was listening to. "Newsflash!" it said. "The LEGO CITY jewellery shop has been robbed. The thieves snatched a priceless necklace! Police roadblocks around the city are causing major traffic delays."

Jett watched jealously as three motorcyclists weaved through the trapped cars. "I wish I'd thought to bring my motorcycle today," he grumbled. Suddenly, he noticed something glittering in the sun. It was a necklace being worn by one of the motorcyclists.

"Whoa!" he laughed. "That's some pretty fancy jewellery to be wearing on a motorcycle ride!"

The motorcyclist at the front was also laughing to himself. "Great idea to use motorcycles for our getaway," he thought. "While the police are stuck in traffic, we can make our escape."

Sting and Ray – the two other members of the School of Sharks gang – pulled up alongside Dan.

Dan noticed the stolen necklace around Sting's neck, and couldn't believe what he was seeing. "Hide those pearls!" he yelled.

"Curls? What curls?" asked Sting, confused. He couldn't hear a thing with his motorcycle helmet on.

Soon, the gang made it to the beach, where Dan unpacked part two of his getaway plan. "Right boys, get changed into these!" he said, grinning wickedly.

"Are those shark costumes?" Ray asked.

"Of course!" replied the smirking Dan. "People are terrified of sharks. No one will dare to chase us with these on. We'll just swim away with the necklace!"

Meanwhile, Jett had finally made it to his plane and started the show. He flew his Super Soarer upside down over the beach, and the crowd cheered.

"That should make up for me being late!" he said, smiling to himself as he saw the crowd's delighted faces.

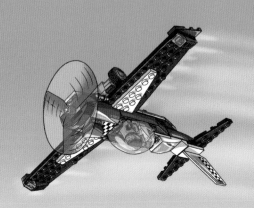

Further along the beach, he spotted an odd sight. "Ha ha! Look at those guys disguised as sharks! What a strange day this is. First the guy wearing a necklace on a motorcycle, and now . . . oh . . . hang on a minute!"

Down below, Jim Rafter nudged his commander. "Look! Jett Powers is skywriting!" "S . . . H . . . A . . . R . . . K . . . G . . . A . . . what does that mean?" asked Sam Stoutheart.

Sam whipped out his binoculars and started scanning the shore. Soon he spotted three shark fins wibbling about in the water.

"A-ha!" he cried. "Now I get it. Rafter – get the dinghy!"

"I think I see what's going on here," Sam said to himself as they approached the 'sharks'. Grabbing an oar, he prodded the closest one and the scowling face of Dan Diddler popped up.

"Rumbled!" Sam grinned. "The School of Sharks gang – who else? It's back to the beach for you three!"

"Since when was it illegal to swim around in a shark costume?" asked Dan once they were back on the beach. He was trying to look innocent.

Sam smiled and pointed up to the sky, where Jett had finished his message.

"'Shark gang," Jim read aloud. "And there's a picture of a necklace next to it."

"We were only trying to give the pearls back to the oysters," Sting whined, desperately hoping the coast guards would believe him. "We thought it would be a nice surprise for them."

"Clam up, guys!" Jim chuckled. With that, Sam snapped on the handcuffs.

HANG ON! IT'S NOT THE END OF THE ADVENTURE YET! FIND OUT WHAT HAPPENS NEXT BY SOLVING THE PUZZLES THAT FOLLOW.

EMERGENCY LANDING

Jett's plane is running out of fuel and needs to land, but the runway is still being built! Number the pieces from one to five so that they can be laid down in the correct order. You'll need to be quick!

KIT CHECK

Sam the coast guard knows what everyone in his team needs to do their job, but each locker is missing at least one vital piece of equipment. Can you work out what the missing items are?

THE BIG RACE

Jim Rafter needs to use lots of different skills to win the annual Coast Guard race. Number each of the pictures below so that they are in the right order.

FINE TUNING

The Monster Truck show is coming to LEGO CITY, and Howie the mechanic has upgraded his favourite vehicle by adding six brand new parts. Can you spot them?

BEFORE:

AFTER:

RECOVERY MISSION

Some LEGO CITY scientists sent a diving chamber under the sea, but it's got stuck under some rocks. Can you find a safe route back up to the surface?

AERIAL ACROBATICS

Only one of the four devices below shows the position of the Super Soarer correctly. Which one is it?

A.

B.

C.

D.

STOWAWAYS!

Three crooks have escaped from prison and are trying to escape by hiding out on the coast guard's boat! Find and circle all three of them, before they get away.

19

SECRET PLAN

At their secret hideaway, the crooks are planning their next robbery – but a police officer can hear everything! Unscramble the code and rearrange the words to find out where the gang are planning to rob next.

CHILD ABOARD!

DANGER! SHARKS!

While flying upside down, Jett can see that the people in the water are surrounded by sharks! Draw just six straight lines between to connect the buoys and protect the tourists.

START

KEY CALAMITY

This stunt driver has lost the key to his monster truck while swimming, so Jim is using sonar to find it. Can you see where it is?

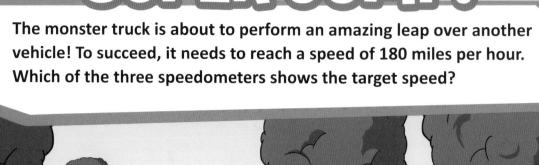

SUPER JUMP!

The monster truck is about to perform an amazing leap over another vehicle! To succeed, it needs to reach a speed of 180 miles per hour. Which of the three speedometers shows the target speed?

A.

B.

C.

LF60055

LIGHTEN THE LOAD

Can you help the LEGO CITY electrician find the quickest route around the broken street lights so that he can fix them? Mark it out for him, avoiding bulbs that work and never going the same way twice.

 – Broken light bulbs

 – Working light bulbs

CUNNING SHARKS

HELP! HELP!

Oh no! Two of the three ropes have come loose from the rescue helicopter's winch. Which of the three castaways will still be pulled to safety?

JUMP TRUCK, JUMP!

The green monster truck is about to attempt an incredible stunt – bouncing all the way to the finish line! Can you figure out his route to the other side?

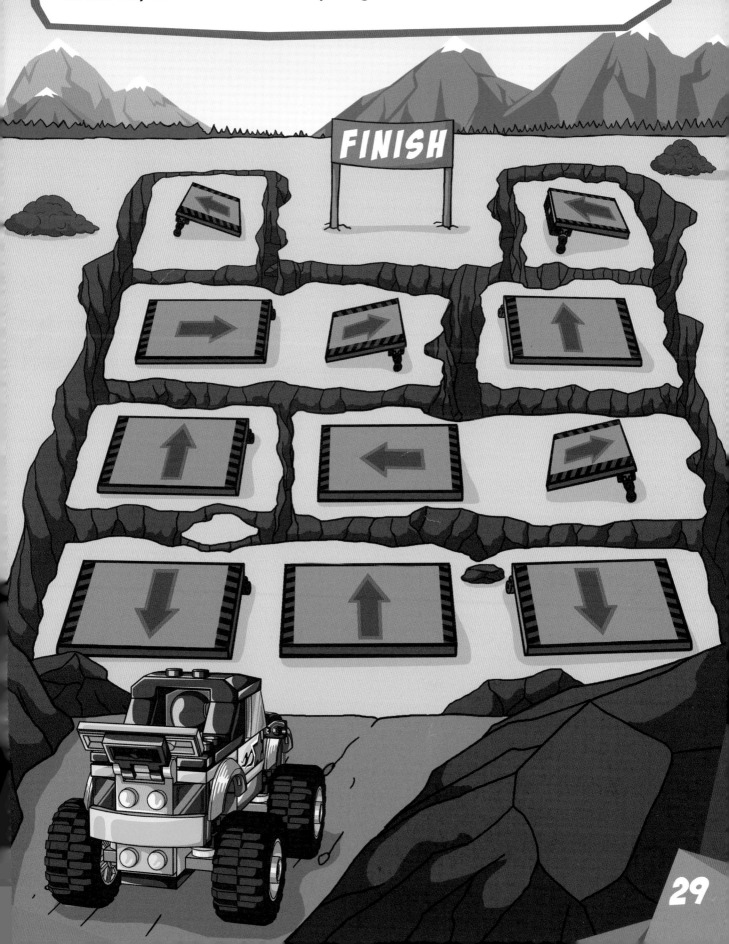

PARTY TIME!

It's the end of a hard day, and the coast guards are having a fancy dress party with their good friends, the stuntmen. Can you see how many of each kind of costume there are?

WATER-THEMED COSTUMES

AIR-THEMED COSTUMES

OTHER COSTUMES